PORTUGUESE
Made Nice & Easy!®

D0096156

Staff of Research & Education Association
Carl Fuchs, Language Program Director

Based on Language Courses developed by the
U.S. Government for Foreign Service Personnel

Research & Education Association
Visit our website at
www.rea.com

Research & Education Association
61 Ethel Road West
Piscataway, New Jersey 08854
E-mail: info@rea.com

PORTUGESE MADE NICE & EASY®

Year 2006 Printing

Printed in the United States of America

Library of Congress Control Number 00-193031

International Standard Book Number 0-87891-375-0

What This Guide Will Do For You

Whether travelling to a foreign country or to your favorite international restaurant, this *Nice & Easy* guide gives you just enough of the language to get around and be understood. Much of the material in this book was developed for government personnel who are often assigned to a foreign country on a moment's notice and need a quick introduction to the language.

In this handy and compact guide, you will find useful words and phrases, popular expressions, common greetings, and the words for numbers, money, and time. Every word or phrase is accompanied with the correct pronunciation and spelling. There is a vocabulary list for finding words quickly.

Generous margins on the pages allow you to make notes and remarks that you may find helpful.

If you expect to travel to Portugal, the section on the country's history and relevant up-to-date facts will make your trip more informative and enjoyable. By keeping this guide with you, you'll be well prepared to understand as well as converse in Portuguese.

Carl Fuchs
Language Program Director

Contents

PORTUGAL

FACTS & HISTORY

Official Name: Portuguese Republic

Geography
Area: 92,391 sq. km., including the Azores and Madeira
Islands; slightly smaller than the State of Indiana.
Cities: Capital - Lisbon (2.5 million), *Other Cities* -
Oporto (1.7 million), Faro.
Terrain: Mountainous in the north; rolling plains in the
central south.

People
Nationality: Portuguese (singular and plural).
Population: 10.6 million.
Population density: 108 per sq. km. (300 per sq. mi.).
Annual growth rate: 0.4%.
Ethnic groups: Homogeneous Mediterranean stock with
small black African and Eastern European minorities.
Religion: Roman Catholic, 97%.
Language: Portuguese.
Education: *Years compulsory* - 9. Literacy - 93%.

Health: *Life expectancy* - 77.5 years.
Work force (5.48 million): *Government and services* -
60%; *industry* - 30%; a*griculture* - 10%.

Government
Type: Republic.
Constitution: Effective April 25, 1976; revised October
30, 1982, June 1, 1989, November 25, 1992, and Sep-
tember 3, 1997.
Branches: *Executive* - president (head of state), Council of
State (presidential advisory body), prime minister (head of
government), Council of Ministers.
Legislative - unicameral Assembly of the Republic (230
deputies). *Judicial* - Supreme Court, district courts, appeals
courts, Constitutional Tribunal.

Economy:
GDP: $188.7 billion.
Annual growth rate: 1.1%.
Natural resources: Fish, tungsten, iron, copper, tin, and
uranium ores. Agriculture: Forestry, fisheries, cork, wine.
Industry: Textiles, clothing, footwear, wood and cork,
paper, chemicals, manufacturing, food and beverages.
Trade: *Exports* - $37.68 billion; clothing, footwear,
machinery, cork and paper products, petroleum, textiles.
Imports - $52.1 billion; machinery, petroleum, textiles,
agricultural products, chemicals.

Portuguese Language

Derived from Latin, the Portuguese language spread along the western coast of the Iberian Peninsula with the Roman invasion of 218 BC. Since then the Portuguese language has been variously influenced and altered, adopting new words used by the Germanic invaders and later, in 711, numerous Arab words after the Moorish invasion of the Peninsula. The result is a language which is spoken in seven countries: Portugal, Brazil, Angola, Mozambique, Guinea-Bissau, São Tomé and Cape Verde, spread over five continents. The Portuguese language is one of the most widely-spoken languages in the world, with 200 million people speaking the language.

In the text of this guide, we have pointed out some differences between the Portuguese of Brazil and Portugal since this guide may be used by visitors to Brazil where Portuguese is spoken by over 160 million people.

History of Portugal

The foundation of Portugal dates back to the year 1143. The stability of its continental borders, which have remained virtually unchanged since the thirteenth century, make Portugal one of the oldest nations in the world, reflecting its distinctive identity and internal unity. In the third quarter of the eighteenth century Portugal began its modernization. In the light of economic interventionism and cultural enlightenment the State structures were reorganized and its trade and industry restructured.

In the transition to the nineteenth century, the winds of change blowing from America and France reached Portugal, putting an end to the traditional monarchy in 1820 and leading to the independence of Brazil and the establishment of a constitutional monarchy in Portugal. The beginning of the twentieth century was marked by an unstable political environment which led to the establishment of the Republic in 1910. Portugal took part in World War I alongside the Allies but by the mid-twenties the country's economic and financial situation was very serious, a situation that eventually brought about the so called "New State," marked by corporatism and authoritarianism, and the suppression of democratic liberties. In April 1974, following a military coup, Portugal again saw the establishment of a democratic regime, which was committed to the country's development and enabled Portugal's accession to the European Economic Community (EEC) in 1986.

It was not until the Romans arrived in the 3rd

century BC that a written record of the Portuguese was begun. It is known, however, that the Iberians settled the peninsula at least 700 or 800 years before the Romans arrived. After 200 years of struggle, Rome finally subdued Iberia in 19 BC and set out to civilize the peninsula. During their half-millennium of control, the Moors introduced a civilization superior in science and culture to that of any country in Europe. They prized literacy and art; encouraged the cultivation of olives, rice, and citrus fruits; introduced Chinese paper-making; resurrected the secret of glass-making; and taught advanced glazing techniques. They also showed a religious tolerance for Muslims, Christians, and Jews, but unfortunately this tolerance did not take hold with Christians when they reclaimed Spain and Portugal.

The Reconquest was launched when the throne of Castile came to Alfonso VI, whose victories prompted the Moors to call on Morocco for assistance. Alfonso, in turn, looked to France for help; a division of knights answered his call, including Henri, a younger son of the Count of Burgundy. Henri's efforts were rewarded with the hand of one of Alfonso's illegitimate daughters and the dowry of the large northwestern territory of Portucale. Henri died young, but his son Afonso Henriques went on to stem another Moorish advance. In 1139 he crowned himself Afonso I, king of Portugal, after refusing to pay homage to

Castile. From that moment on, with the exception of a 60-year hiatus, Portugal has been independent of Spain.

Initially, Afonso's kingdom consisted only of the northern third of modern Portugal. The rest of the country was controlled by Moors, but Afonso managed to retake Lisbon and much of the south. After his death in 1185, his son and grandson carried on the campaign, regaining all of modern-day Portugal except for scattered pockets of Moorish controlled land. When these were finally conquered by 1249, Portugal became the first unified country in Europe. The first king after pacification was complete was Dinis I, who granted land to the common farmer and founded Portugal's first university. It was during his reign that most of the great fortresses were completed that still guard Portugal's eastern border against Spain. Two reigns later Pedro I occupied the throne. Pedro sired a number of illegitimate children, one of whom he installed as the abbot of the religio-military order of Avís, an organization that resembled the Knights Templar. That abbot would one day seize the crown.

Fernando I succeeded Pedro, but died early. His widow, Leonor Teles, took up residence with a courtier, married off Fernando's daughter Beatrice to the king of Castile, and then went on to send heralds throughout the land announcing that the king of

Castile ruled Portugal. This prompted the abbot Master of the Order of Avís to do away with Leonor's paramour and, in 1385, have himself proclaimed king of Portugal. However, it was one thing for João I to take the crown, and quite another to convince the king of Castile to give up his claim to Portugal. The two met in battle on the plains of Aljubarrota north of Lisbon, where João miraculously won the day. To commemorate this victory, he constructed the great monastery at Batalha. João married Philippa of Lancaster. Their four sons joined in an invasion of Ceuta on the Moroccan coast, and one son—Dom Henrique—devoted his life to encouraging maritime exploration, for which he became known as "Prince Henry the Navigator." He financed expeditions that discovered Madeira and the Azore Islands (still territories of Portugal today) and made their way down most of the African coast.

In 1495 the throne came to the son of an adopted child of Prince Henry. Manuel I presided over many of the great Portuguese discoveries, including Vasco da Gama's voyage to India and Pedro Cabral's discovery of Brazil. Thanks to its outposts throughout Africa, India, and the Far East, from which it imported spices, tea, and coffee, for a brief moment Portugal was the richest country in Europe. When the last Avís died childless, Felipe II of Spain gained the throne, and Spain ruled Portugal. Sixty years later, Felipe's descendent appointed Spaniards to government positions, inciting the Portuguese. The powerful Duke of Bragança was especially feared by the Spanish as a rallying point for Portuguese rebellion at this time. When the Spanish tried to seduce the duke by giving him control of the Portuguese army, Bragança turned his troops against them and conquered all of Portugal in a matter of weeks. Thus did João IV found the Bragança dynasty, Portugal's last. In 1706 João V came to the throne. He built ostentatiously throughout Portugal, funding his projects with gold and diamonds discovered in Brazil; especially splendid is the palace at Mafra, near Lisbon, and the library at Coimbra. His son, José I, lacked all ambition and allowed a favorite minister named Pombal to rule the country. It was Pombal who stepped forward to resurrect Lisbon when the city was leveled by the great earthquake of 1755.

Since 1386, Portugal had been tied by a treaty of friendship with England, so when Napoléon declared war on England, Portugal found herself embroiled in the conflict. Napoléon's troops invaded in 1808, and a year later England sent the future Duke of Wellington to drive them out. The Portuguese royals had, however, fled to Brazil, where they remained for another decade, even though Wellington had chased the French from Portugal by 1811 and from Spain two years later. When the king returned to Portugal in 1821, he found that a constitution rejecting absolute rule had been drafted in his absence. The monarchy refused to acknowledge this, however, and in 1908 the king and his heir were assassinated. One king would follow, but an uprising by the navy sent him into exile in 1910, making Portugal a republic at last.

With no democratic tradition, Portugal had a stormy time with republican government, switching ministers and parties several times a year. The economy concurrently deteriorated, exacerbated by the cost of joining the Allies in World War I. By 1925, three separate military coups had been attempted, and in 1926 one was successful. António de Oliveira Salazar, an economics professor, was appointed prime minister by 1932. He then promulgated a new constitution in which only his party could field candidates, making him de facto dictator. Salazar kept Portugal out of WWII, from which it profited greatly, but by the 1960s economic troubles brewed again. Independence movements in the African colonies of Angola, Mozambique, and Guinea could not be quelled. During this crisis, Salazar suffered an incapacitating stroke—he died two years later in 1970. President Américo Tomás replaced Salazar with party faithful Marcelo, who tried to hold on to the African colonies with 50,000 Portuguese troops, a huge drain for the small country.

The army itself finally revolted in 1974, filling the

streets of Lisbon with flower-draped tanks in the so-called "Flower Revolution." One general recognized the futility of military colonization in Africa and subsequently became president; freeing the colonies was his first official act. Today Portugal is set on a moderate socialist course. Religion: Freedom of conscience, of religion, and of worship are granted by the constitution of the Republic. The churches and religious communities are independent and separate from the State. For historical reasons dating back to the foundation of the Portuguese nation, the Catholic church still plays a dominant role nowadays.

Almural Castle

Church in Braga

2

Algarve coast

Hints on Pronunciation

The words and phrases in this *Guide* are written in a spelling which you read like English. When you see the word for *fruit* spelled *FROO-tahss*, give the *oo* the sound it has in the English words *too, boot,* etc. Each letter or combination of letters is used for the sound it usually stands for in English and it *always* stands for that sound. Thus, *oo* is always pronounced as it is in *too, boot, tooth, roost,* never as anything else. Say these words and then pronounce the vowel by itself. That is the sound you must use every time you see *oo* in the *Pronunciation* column.

Detail, Jeronimos Monastery, Lisbon

Syllables that are accented, that is, pronounced louder than others, are written in capital letters. In Portugal unaccented syllables are skipped over very quickly, just as they are in English, but in Brazil they are pronounced more evenly and clearly. In both Brazil and Portugal you will notice that unaccented -*ee* and -*oo* at the end of a word often disappear or sound as though they are being whispered rather than spoken out loud.

Curved lines (‿) are used to show sounds that are pronounced together without any break; for example, *NA‿oong* meaning "no," *L‿YEE* meaning "you."

Special Points

EH   as in *let, bed, ten*. Examples: *EH* meaning "is," *KEH-roo* meaning "I want."

AY   as in *may, say, play* but don't drawl it out as we do in English. Example: *TRAYSS* meaning "three."

J   stands for the sound we have in *measure, usual, division, occasion*. We have no single letter for this sound in English, so we write it in this *Guide* as *j*. Remember that *j* always stands for the sound in *measure*, never for the sound in *judge*. Example: *O-jee* meaning "today."

NG, N *and* M   are written after certain vowels to show that they are pronounced through the nose. Remember that the *ng, n* and *m* are there only to remind you to pronounce the vowels through the nose. Examples: *BAWNG* meaning "good," *SEENG* meaning "yes," *NA‿oong* meaning "no," *OONG* meaning "one," *een-TEN-doo* meaning "I understand," *kwa-REN-ta* meaning "forty."

RR   is pronounced in two ways: in Portugal you hear a strongly rolled *r*-sound, somewhat like the telephone operator's "thuh-r-r-ree" for "three" or like the Scotchman's "burr" in pronouncing "very" as "ve-r-r-ry." In

5

Brazil you find both this pronunciation and, more frequently, another pronunciation which is very much like the sound you make when you gargle. The double *rr* is different from the single *r* which is made by a quick tap of the tongue against the gums back of the teeth. Example of *rr: see-GA-rrooss* meaning "cigarettes." Example of *r: pawr fa-VAWR* meaning "please."

DJ

stands for the sound we have in *judge*. It is heard in certain parts of Brazil in words like *AWN-djee* meaning "where" and *DJEE-a* meaning "day." Elsewhere these words are pronounced *AWN-dee* and *DEE-a*.

CH

stands for the sound of *ch* in *church*. It is heard in certain parts of Brazil in words like *LAY-chee* meaning "milk" and *VEEN-chee* meaning "twenty." Elsewhere these words are pronounced *LAY-tee* and *VEEN-tee*.

Pena Pálace, Sintra

Ponta Delgada Cathedral, São Miguel, Açores

USEFUL WORDS AND PHRASES

GREETINGS AND GENERAL PHRASES

English	*Pronunciation and Regular Spelling*
Good day	*bawng DJEE-a* (Bom dia)
Good evening	*BO-a TAR-dee* (Boa tarde)
Sir	*sayn-YAWR* (Senhor)
Madam	*sayn-YAW-ra* (Senhora)
Miss	*sayn-yo-REE-ta* (Senhorita)

The Brazilians use a phrase meaning "please" and they use it often. What they say is *pawr fa-VAWR*.

Monastery of Batalha, Lisbon

English	Pronunciation and Regular Spelling
Please	*pawr fa-VAWR* (Por favor)
Excuse me	*day-SKOOL-pee mee* (Desculpe me)
Thank you	*o-bree-GA-doo* (Obrigado)
Yes	*SEENG* (Sim)

"No" is pronounced like the English word "now" spoken through the nose.

No	*NA⌣oong* (Não)
Understand me?	*een-TEN-dee mee?* (Entende me?)
I don't understand	*NA⌣oong een-TEN-doo* (Não entendo)
Please speak slowly	*pawr fa-VAWR, FA-lee dee-va-GAR* (Por favor, fale devagar)

LOCATION

When you need directions to get some place you use the phrase "Where is"; then add the words you need.

Where is	*AWN-djee AH* (Onde há)
a restaurant	*oong rray-sto-RAHNG* (um restaurant)
Where is a restaurant?	*AWN-djee AH oong rray-sto-RAHNG?* (Onde há um restaurant?)

English	*Pronunciation and Regular Spelling*
a hotel	*oong o-TEL* (um hotel)
Where is a hotel?	*AWN-djee AH oong o-TEL?* (Onde há um hotel?)
a railroad	*ah ee-STRA-da djee FEH-rroo* (a estrada de ferro)
Where is a railroad?	*AWN-djee EH ah ee-STRA-da djee FEH-rroo?* (Onde é a estrada de ferro?)
a toilet	*ah pree-VA-da* (a privada)
Where is a toilet?	*AWN-djee EH ah pree-VA-da?* (Onde é a privada?)

Hilltop castle, Sesimbra

10

DIRECTIONS

The answer to your question "Where is such and such?" may be "Turn right" or "Turn left" or "Straight ahead," so you need to know these phrases.

Turn right   *VEE-ree ah djee-RAY-ta*   (Vire à direita)

Turn left   *VEE-ree ah ee-SKAYR-da*   (Vire à
                                                    esquerda)

Straight ahead *SEE-ga eeng FREN-chee*   (Siga em frente)

It is sometimes useful to say "Please point."

Please point   *pawr fa-VAWR, MAW-stree*   (Por favor,
                                                        mostre)

If you are driving and ask the distance to another town, it will be given you in kilometers, not miles.

Kilometers   *kee-LO-may-trooss*   (quilómetros)

One kilometer equals ⅝ of a mile.

NUMBERS

You need to know the numbers.

One   *OONG*   um

Two   *DOYSS*   dois

English	Pronunciation and Regular Spelling	
Three	*TRAYSS*	três
Four	*KWA-troo*	quatro
Five	*SEEN-koo*	cinco

OONG, DOYSS, TRAYSS, KWA-troo, SEEN-koo

Five kilometers	*SEEN-koo* *kee-LO-may-trooss*	cinco quilómetros

Six	*SAYSS*	seis
Seven	*SECH-ee*	sete
Eight	*OY-too*	oito
Nine	*NAW-vee*	nove
Ten	*DAYSS*	dez

SAYSS, SECH-ee, OY-too, NAW-vee, DAYSS

Ten kilometers	*DAYSS* *kee-LO-may-trooss*	dez quilómetros

For the numbers "eleven" through "fifteen" you add an ending which sounds like *ZEE*.

Eleven	*AWN-zee*	onze
Twelve	*DO-zee*	doze

12

English	Pronunciation and Regular Spelling	
Thirteen	*TRAY-zee*	treze
Fourteen	*kwa-TAWR-zee*	quatorze
Fifteen	*KEEN-zee*	quinze

AWN-zee, DO-zee, TRAY-zee, kwa-TAWR-zee, KEEN-zee

For the numbers "sixteen" through "nineteen" you put *DJEE-zeh* before "six," "seven," "eight" and "nine." For example:

Sixteen	*djee-zeh-SAYSS*	dezesseis
Seventeen	*djee-zeh-SECH-ee*	dezessete
		(and so on)
Twenty	*VEEN-chee*	vinte

To this you add "one"—*OONG*—to make "twenty-one," or "two"—*DOYSS*—to make "twenty-two" and so on.

Twenty-one	*VEEN-chee ee OONG*	
		vinte e um
Twenty-two	*VEEN-chee ee DOYSS*	
		vinte e dois
		(and so on)

13

You add the numbers "one" through "nine" in the same way you did in the twenties to make "thirty-one," "thirty-two" and so on.

The numbers "forty," "fifty," "sixty," "seventy," "eighty" and "ninety" all end in *EN-ta*.

Forty	*kwa-REN-ta*	quarenta
Fifty	*seen-KWEN-ta*	cinquenta (and so on)
One hundred	*SAYNG*	cem
One thousand	*MEEL*	mil

WHAT'S THAT?

When you want to know the name of something you can say "What's that?" and point to the thing you mean.

What is	*o kee EH*	(O que é)
that	*a-KEE-loo*	(aquilo)
What is that?	*o kee EH a-KEE-loo?*	(O que é aquilo?)

Town of Sintra

English	*Pronunciation and Regular Spelling*

ASKING FOR THINGS

When you want something use the phrase "I want" and add the name of the thing wanted. Always say "please"—*pawr fa-VAWR*.

I want   *KEH-roo*   (Quero)

  cigarettes   *see-GA-rrooss*   (cigarros)

15

English	Pronunciation and Regular Spelling
Please, I want cigarettes	*pawr fa-VAWR, KEH-roo see-GA-rrooss* (Por favor, quero cigarros)
to eat	*koo-MAYR* (comer)
Please, I want to eat	*pawr fa-VAWR, KEH-roo koo-MAYR* (Por favor, quero comer)

Here are some of the words for things you may require.

bread	*PA‿oong*	(pão)
fruit	*FROO-tahss*	(frutas)
water	*AH-gwa*	(água)
eggs	*AW-vooss*	(óvos)
beefsteak	*BEE-fee*	(bife)
potatoes	*ba-TA-tahss*	(batatas)
rice	*a-RROYSS*	(arroz)
beans	*fay-JA‿oong*	(feijão)
fish	*PAY-shee*	(peixe)
salad	*sa-LA-da*	(salada)
milk	*LAY-chee*	(leite)
beer	*sayr-VAY-ja*	(cerveja)

16

English	Pronunciation and Regular Spelling
a glass of beer	*oong KAW-poo djee sayr-VAY-ja* (um copo de cerveja)
coffee	*ka-FEH* (café)
a cup of coffee	*oo-ma SHEE-ka-ra djee ka-FEH* (uma chicara de café)

MONEY

To find out how much things cost you say:

How much?   *KWAHN-too KOO-sta?*   Quanto custa?

Cascais

17

TIME

To find out what time it is you say:

What time   *kee AW-rahss SA‿oong?*   (Que horas são?)
is it?

Quarter past five is said in Brazilian "five and a quarter."

Quarter past   *SEEN-koo ee oong KWAR-too*   (cinco e
five   um quarto)

Half past six is said "six and a half."

Half past six   *SAYSS ee MAY-ya*   (seis e meia)

Twenty minutes past seven is said "seven and twenty"—the hour plus the number of minutes.

Twenty past   *SECH-ee ee VEEN-chee*   (sete e vinte)
seven

To say "quarter of" or "ten minutes of," the Brazilian is:

A quarter of   *oong KWAR-too pa-ra*   (um quarto para)

Quarter of two   *oong KWAR-too pa-ra ahz DOO-ahss*
                                          (um quarto para as duas)

English	Pronunciation and Regular Spelling

Ten minutes of three in Brazilian is said "ten to three."

Ten minutes of three   *DAYSS pa-ra ahss TRAYSS*   (dez para as três)

If you want to know when a movie starts or when a train leaves you say:

At what time   *ah kee AW-rahss*   (A que horas)

the movie   *oo see-NAY-ma*   (o cinema)

starts   *koo-MESS-a*   (começa)

At what time does the movie start?   *ah kee AW-rahss koo-MESS-a oo see-NAY-ma?*   (A que horas começa o cinema?)

the train   *oo TRAYNG*   (o trem)

leave   *SA‿ee*   (sai)

At what time does the train leave?   *ah kee AW-rahss SA‿ee oo TRAYNG?*   (A que horas sai o trem?)

Today   *O-jee*   (hoje)

Tomorrow   *a-mahn-YAHNG*   (amanhã)

English	Pronunciation and Regular Spelling

The days of the week are:

Sunday	*do-MEEN-goo* (Domingo)
Monday	*say-goon-da-FAY-ra* (Segunda-Feira)
Tuesday	*tehr-sa-FAY-ra* (Terça-Feira)
Wednesday	*kwar-ta-FAY-ra* (Quarta-Feira)
Thursday	*keen-ta-FAY-ra* (Quinta-Feira)
Friday	*sayss-ta-FAY-ra* (Sexta-Feira)
Saturday	*SA-ba-doo* (Sábado)

OTHER USEFUL PHRASES

The following phrases will also be useful.

What is your name? *KO-moo say SHA-ma?* (Como se chama?)

My name is___ *may‿oo NO-mee EH___* (Meu nome é___)

Does anyone here speak English? *ahl-GAYNG a-KEE FA-la een-GLAYSS?* (Alguem aquí fala inglês?)

Please write it *pawr fa-VAWR, ay-SKRAY-va-o* (Por favor, escreva-o)

English	Pronunciation and Regular Spelling
Until to-morrow	*a-TEH a-mahn-YAHNG* (Até amanhã)
Good-by	*a-TEH LAW-goo* (Até logo)

Archway, Lisbon

ADDITIONAL EXPRESSIONS

English	Pronunciation and Regular Spelling
How do you say____?	*KO-moo see DEESS____?* (Como se diz____?)
in Brazilian	*eeng bra-zee-YAY-roo* (em brasileiro)
in Portuguese	*eeng pawr-too-GAYSS* (em português)
Stop!	*PA-reel* (Pare!)
Come here!	*VAYN-ya KA!* (Venha cá!)
Quickly	*dee-PRESS-a* (Depressa)
Come quickly!	*VAYN-ya dee-PRESS-a!* (Venha depressa!)
Go quickly!	*VA dee-PRESS-a!* (Vá depressa!)
Help!	*so-KO-rrool* (Socorro!)
Help me!	*a-JOO-dee-mee!* (Ajude-me!)
Bring help!	*TRA-ga a‿oo-SEEL-yoo!* (Traga auxílio!)
I will pay you	*AY‿oo l‿yee pa-ga-RAY* (Eu lhe pagarei)
I am an American	*SO a-may-ree-KA-noo* (Sou americano)
I am your friend	*SO a-MEE-goo* (Sou amigo)
How far is the town?	*ah kee dee-STAHNSS-ya FEE-ka ah see-DA-dee?* (A que distância fica a cidade?)

22

English	Pronunciation and Regular Spelling
How far is it?	*ah kee dee-STAHNSS-ya FEE-ka?* (Á que distância fica?)
Where is it?	*AWN-dee EH?* (Onde é?)
Is it far?	*eh LAWN-jee?* (E longe?)
It is near	*eh PAYR-too* (É perto)
Which way is north?	*dee kee LA-doo EH oo NAWR-tee?* (De que lado é o norte?)
Which is the road to___?	*KWAHL EH ah ee-STRA-da pa-ra___?* (Qual é a estrada para___?)
Draw me a map	*day-ZAYN-yee oong MA-pa* (Desenhe um mapa)
Take me there	*LEV-ee-mee a-TEH LA* (Leve-me até lá)
Take me to a doctor	*LEV-ee-mee ah oong MED-ee-koo* (Leve-me a um médico)
Take me to the hospital	*LEV-ee-mee a_oo aw-spee-TAHL* (Leve-me ao hospital)
Danger!	*pee-REE-goo!* (Perigo!)

Jeronimos Monastery, Lisbon

Pousada de Alvito

English	Pronunciation and Regular Spelling
Watch out!	*a-ten-SA⌣oong!* (Atenção!)
Gas!	*GAHSS!* (Gás!)
Take cover!	*a-BREE-gee-zee!* (Abrigue-se!)
Wait a minute!	*ee-SPEH-roo oong een-STAHN-teel* (Espere um instante!)
Good luck	*fee-lee-see-DA-deess* (Felicidades)

24

FILL-IN SENTENCES

In this section you will find a number of sentences, each containing a blank space which can be filled in with any of the words in the list that follows. For example, in order to say "Where can I get some soap?" look for the phrase "Where can I get___?" in the English column and find the expression given beside it: *AWN-dee paw-day-RAY awb-TAYR___?* Then look for "soap" in the list that follows; it is *sa-BA͜-oong.* Put the word for "soap" in the blank space and you get *AWN-dee paw-day-RAY awb-TAYR sa͜BA-oong?*

English	Pronunciation and Regular Spelling
I want___	*KEH-roo___* (Quero___)
I'd like___	*day-ZAY-joo___* (Desejo___)
We want___	*kay-RAY-mooss___* (Queremos___)
Give me___	*DAY-mee___* (Dê-me___)
Bring me___	*TRA-ga-mee___* (Traga-me___)
Where can I get___?	*AWN-dee paw-day-RAY awb-TAYR___?* (Onde poderei obter___?)
I have___	*TAYN-yoo___* (Tenho___)
I don't have___	*NA͜oong TAYN-yoo___* (Não tenho___)
We have___	*TAY-mooss___* (Temos___)

English	Pronunciation and Regular Spelling
We don't have___	*NA⌣oong TAY-mooss___* (Não temos___)
Have you___?	*TAYNG___?* (Tem___?)

EXAMPLE

I want___	*KEH-roo___* (Quero___)	
food	*koo-MEE-da* (comida)	
I want food	*KEH-roo koo-MEE-da* (Quero comida)	

apples	*ma-SA⌣eenss* (maçãs)	
bacon	*to-SEEN-yoo* (toucinho)	
bananas	*ba-NA-nahss* (bananas)	
boiled water	*AH-gwa fayr-VEE-da* (agua fervida)	
butter	*mahn-TAY-ga* (manteiga)	
cabbage	*rray-POHL-yoo* (repolho)	
carrots	*see-NO-rahss* (cenouras)	
chicken	*FRAHN-goo* (frango)	
chocolate	*sho-ko-LA-tee* (chocolate)	
cucumbers	*pee-PEE-nooss* (pepinos)	
grapes	*OO-vahss* (uvas)	

English	Pronunciation and Regular Spelling
ham	*pree-ZOON-too* (presunto)
ice cream	*sawr-VAY-tee* (sorvête)
lamb	*kar-NAY-roo* (carneiro)
lemons	*lee-MOYNSS* (limões)
lettuce	*ahl-FA-see* (alface)
mangos	*MAHN-gahss* (mangas)
onions	*see-BO-lahss* (cebôlas)
oranges	*la-RAHN-jahss* (laranjas)
peas	*ayr-VEEL-yahss* (ervilhas)
pepper	*pee-MEN-ta* (pimenta)
pineapple *or in Portugal*	*a-BA-ka-shee* (abacaxi) *AH-na-nahss* (ananás)
pork	*PAWR-koo* (porco)
salt	*SAHL* (sal)
soup	*SO-pa* (sôpa)
sugar	*a-SOO-kar* (açúcar)
tea	*SHA* (chá)
tomatoes	*to-MA-teess* (tomates)
veal	*vee-TEL-a* (vitela)

English	Pronunciation and Regular Spelling
vegetables	*vej-eh-TA gess* (vegetais)
wine	*VEEN-yoo* (vinho)

(For other foods see pages 16 and 17.)

a cup	*oo-ma SHEE-ka-ra* (uma chícara)
a fork	*oong GAR-foo* (um garfo)
a glass	*oong KAW-poo* (um copo)
a knife	*oo-ma FA-ka* (uma faca)
a plate	*oong PRA-too* (um prato)
a spoon	*oo-ma kool-YAYR* (uma colher)
a bed	*oo-ma KA-ma* (uma cama)
blankets	*koo-bayr-TAW-reess* (cobertores)
a mattress	*oong kawl-SHA oong* (um colchão)
a mosquito net	*oong mooss-kee-TAY-roo* (um mosquiteiro)
a pillow	*oong tra-vee-SAY-roo* (um travesseiro)
a room	*oong KWAR-too* (um quarto)
sheets	*len-SOYSS* (lençóis)

English	Pronunciation and Regular Spelling
cigars	*sha-ROO-tooss* (charutos)
matches	*FAW-sfaw-rooss* (fósforos)
a pipe	*oong ka-SHEEM-boo* (um cachimbo)
tobacco *or in Portugal*	*FOO-moo* (fumo) *ta-BA-koo* (tabaco)
ink	*TEEN-ta* (tinta)
paper	*pa-PEL* (papel)
a pen	*oo-ma ka-NET-a* (uma caneta)
a pencil	*oong LA-peess* (um lápis)
a comb	*oong PEN-tee* (um pente)
hot water	*AH-gwa KEN-tee* (agua quente)
a razor	*oo-ma na-VAHL-ya* (uma navalha)
razor blades	*LA-mee-nahss dee jee-LET-ee* (lâminas de gilete)
a shaving brush	*oong peen-SEL dee BAR-ba* (um pincel de barba)
shaving soap	*sa-BA⌣oong dee BAR-ba* (sabão de barba)
soap	*sa-BA⌣oong* (sabão)

English	Pronunciation and Regular Spelling
a tooth-brush	*oo-ma ee-SKO-va dee DEN-teess* (uma escova de dentes)
tooth paste	*PA-sta pa-ra DEN-teess* (pasta para dentes)
a towel	*oo-ma TWAHL-ya* (uma toalha)
a handker-chief	*oong LEN-soo* (um lenço)
a raincoat	*oong eem-payr-mee-AH-vel* (um impermeável)
a shirt	*oo-ma ka-MEE-za* (uma camisa)
shoe laces	*kawr-DOYNSS dee sa-PA-tooss* (cordões de sapatos)
shoe polish	*GRA-sha dee sa-PA-too* (graxa de sapato)
shoes	*sa-PA-tooss* (sapatos)
undershirt	*oo-ma ka-mee-ZAY-ta* (uma camiseta)
undershorts	*KWEK-ahss* (cuécas)
buttons	*boo-TOYNSS* (botões)
a needle	*oo-ma a-GOOL-ya* (uma agulha)
safety pins	*ahl-fee-NAY-tee dee see-goo-RAHN-sa* (alfinete de segurança)
thread	*LEEN-ya* (linha)

English	Pronunciation and Regular Spelling
adhesive tape	*ay-spa-ra-DRA-poo* (esparadrapo)
or in Portugal	*ahd-SEE-voo* (adesivo)
aspirin	*a-spee-REE-na* (aspirina)
a bandage	*oo-ma a-ta-DOO-ra* (uma atadura)
or in Portugal	*oo-ma lee-ga-DOO-ra* (uma ligadura)
cotton	*ahl-goo-DA ͜oong* (algodão)
a disinfectant	*oong dee-ZEEN-fay-tahn-tee* (um desinfetante)
a laxative	*oong poor-GAHN-tee* (um purgante)
gasoline	*ga-zo-LEE-na* (gasolina)

I want to__	*KEH-roo___* (Quero___)

EXAMPLE

I want to__	*KEH-roo___* (Quero___)
sleep	*door-MEER* (dormir)
I want to sleep	*KEH-roo door-MEER* (Quero dormir)

be shaved	*fa-ZAYR ah BAR-ba* (fazer a barba)

English	Pronunciation and Regular Spelling
drink	*bay-BAYR* (beber)
have my hair cut	*kawr-TAR oo ka-BAY-loo* (cortar o cabêlo)
rest	*dee-skahn-SAR* (descançar)
take a bath	*too-MAR BAHN-yoo* (tomar banho)
wash	*la-VAR* (lavar)

Where is there___?	*AWN-dee AH___?* (Onde há___?)
Where can I find___?	*AWN-dee PAW-soo een-kawn-TRAR___?* (Onde posso encontrar___?)

EXAMPLE

Where is there___?	*AWN-dee AH___?* (Onde há___?)
a barber	*oong bar-BAY-roo* (um barbeiro)
Where is there a barber?	*AWN-dee AH oong bar-BAY-roo?* (Onde há um barbeiro?)

a barber	*oong bar-BAY-roo* (um barbeiro)
a dentist	*oong den-TEE-sta* (um dentista)
a doctor	*oong MED-ee-koo* (um médico)

32

English	Pronunciation and Regular Spelling
a mechanic	*oong may-KA-nee-koo* (um mecânico)
a policeman	*oong poo-LEESS-ya* (um polícia)
a porter	*oong ka-rreh-ga-DAWR* (um carregador)
a servant	*oong kree-AH-doo* (um criado)
a shoemaker	*oong sa-pa-TAY-roo* (um sapateiro)
a tailor	*oong ahl-fa-YA-tee* (um alfaiate)
a workman	*oong tra-bahl-ya-DAWR* (um trabalhador)

a church	*oo-ma ee-GRAY-ja* (uma igreja)
a clothing store	*oo-ma ahl-fa-ya-ta-REE-a* (uma alfaiataria)
a drugstore	*oo-ma far-MAHSS-ya* (uma farmácia)
a garage	*oo-ma ga-RAHJ* (uma garage)
a grocery store	*oo-ma VEN-da* (uma venda)
a house	*oo-ma KA-za* (uma casa)
a laundry	*oo-ma la-vahn-da-REE-a* (uma lavandaria)
a spring	*oo-ma FAWN-tee* (uma fonte)

33

English	Pronunciation and Regular Spelling
Where is___?	*A WN-dee EH___?* (Onde é___?)
How far is___?	*ah kee dee-STAHNSS-ya FEE-ka___?*
	(A que distância fica___?)

EXAMPLE

Where is___?	*A WN-dee EH___?* (Onde é___?)
the bridge	*ah PA WN-tee* (a ponte)
Where is the bridge?	*A WN-dee EH ah PA WN-tee?* (Onde é a ponte?)

the bus	*oo AW-nee-booss* (o ônibus)
the camp	*oo a-kahm-pa-MEN-too* (o acampamento)
the city	*ah see-DA-dee* (a cidade)
the highway	*ah ee-STRA-da preen-see-PAHL* (a estrada principal)
the hospital	*oo aw-spee-TAHL* (o hospital)
the main street	*ah RROO-a preen-see-PAHL* (a rua principal)
the market	*oo mayr-KA-doo* (o mercado)
the nearest town	*ah see-DA-dee MA⏝eess PRA W-see-ma* (a cidade mais próxima)

English	Pronunciation and Regular Spelling
the police station	*ah day-lay-ga-SEE-a dee poo-LEESS-ya* (a delegacia de polícia)
the post office	*oo kaw-RRAY-oo* (o correio)
the railroad station	*ah ee-sta-SA͜oong* (a estação)
the river	*oo RREE-oo* (o rio)
the road	*ah ee-STRA-da* (a estrada)
the street car	*oo BAWN-dee* (o bonde)
or in Portugal	*oo ee-LET-ree-koo* (o elétrico)
the telegraph office	*oo tay-LEG-ra-foo* (o telégrafo)
the telephone	*oo tay-lay-FAW-nee* (o telefóne)
the village	*ah VEE-la* (a vila)

I am___	*ee-STO___* (Estou___)
He is___	*ee-STA___* (Está___)

EXAMPLE

I am___	*ee-STO___* (Estou___)
sick	*DWEN-tee* (doente)
I am sick	*ee-STO DWEN-tee* (Estou doente)

35

English	Pronunciation and Regular Spelling
hungry	*kawng FAW-mee* (com fome)
lost	*payr-DEE-doo* (perdido)
thirsty	*kawng SAY-dee* (com sêde)
tired	*kahn-SA-doo* (cançado)
well	*BAYNG* (bem)
wounded	*fee-REE-doo* (ferido)

We are___	*ee-STA-mooss___* (Estamos___)
They are___	*ee-STA⌣oong___* (Estão___)
Are you___?	*ee-STA___?* (Está___?)

EXAMPLE

We are___	*ee-STA-mooss___* (Estamos___)
wounded	*fee-REE-dooss* (feridos)
We are wounded	*ee-STA-mooss fee-REE-dooss* (Estamos feridos)
hungry	*kawng FAW-mee* (com fome)
lost	*payr-DEE-dooss* (perdidos)
sick	*DWEN-tee* (doente)

English	Pronunciation and Regular Spelling
thirsty	*kawng SAY-dee* (com sêde)
tired	*kahn-SA-dooss* (cancados)
well	*BAYNG* (bem)

Is it___?	*ee-STA___?* (Está___?)
It is___.	*ee-STA___* (Está___)
This is___	*EE-stoo ee-STA___* (Isto está___)

Minhos

English	Pronunciation and Regular Spelling
That is____	*a-KEE-loo ee-STA*____ (Aquilo está____)
It is not____	*NA‿oong ee-STA*____ (Não está____)
It is too____ It is very____ }	*ee-STA MOO‿een-too*____ (Está muito____)

EXAMPLE

It is____	*ee-STA*____ (Está____)
clean	*LEEM-poo* (limpo)
It is clean	*ee-STA LEEM-poo* (Está limpo)
dirty	*SOO-joo* (sujo)
cold	*FREE-oo* (frio)
warm *or* hot	*KEN-tee* (quente)

Is it____?	*EH*____? (É____?)
It is____	*EH*____ (É____)
This is____	*EE-sto eh*____ (Isto é____)
That is____	*a-KEE-loo eh* (Aquilo é____)
It is not____	*NA‿oong eh*____ (Não é____)
It is too____ It is very____ }	*eh MOO‿een-too*____ (É muito____)

38

English	Pronunciation and Regular Spelling
	EXAMPLE
This is____	*EE-stoo eh____* (Isto é____)
good	*BAWNG* (bom)
This is good	*EE-stoo eh BAWNG* (Isto é bom)
bad	*MA‿oo* (mau)
large	*GRAHN-dee* (grande)
small	*pee-KEN-oo* (pequeno)
cheap	*ba-RA-too* (barato)
expensive	*KA-roo* (caro)
enough	*ba-STAHN-tee* (bastante)
much	*MOO‿een-too* (muito)
near	*PAYR-too* (perto)
far	*LAWN-jee* (longe)
here	*a-KEE* (aqui)
there	*a-LEE* (ali)

NOTE

The last two sets of Fill-In Sentences are listed separately because there are two different words for "is" in Brazilian and Portuguese.

IMPORTANT SIGNS

Pare	Stop
Vá devagar	Go Slow
Perigo	Danger
Um só sentido	One Way
Não é passagem	No Thoroughfare
Conserve a direita	Keep to the Right
Estrada em construção	Road under Construction
Curva perigosa	Dangerous Curve
Pare a 300 metros	Stop at 300 Meters
Atenção á locomotiva	Look Out for Locomotive
Linhas de alta tensão	High Tension Lines
Travessia perigosa	Dangerous Crossing
Estacionamento proíbido	No Parking
Entrada proíbida	No Admittance
É proíbido fumar	No Smoking
Senhoras	Women
Homens	Men
Entrada	Entrance
Saída	Exit

ALPHABETICAL WORD LIST

English	*Pronunciation and Regular Spelling*

A

a
oong (um)
or *oo-ma* (uma)

adhesive tape   *ay-spa-ra-DRA-poo*   (esparadrapo)
or in Portugal *ahd-SEE-voo*   (adesivo)

am

  I am
    ee-STO___ (Estou___)
    or *SO___* (Sou___)

American   *a-may-ree-KA-noo* (americano)

  Americans   *a-may-ree-KA-nooss* (americanos)

  American   *sohl-DA-dooss a-may-ree-KA-nooss*
  soldiers   (soldados Americanos)

and   *ee* (e)

anyone   *ahl-GAYNG* (alguem)

apples   *ma-SA‿eenss* (maçãs)

are

  Are you___?   *ee-STA___?* (Está___?)

  They are___   *ee-STA‿oong___* (Estão___)

  We are___   *ee-STA-mooss___* (Estamos___)

aspirin   *a-spee-REE-na* (aspirina)

41

English	Pronunciation and Regular Spelling

B

bacon	*to-SEEN-yoo* (toucinho)
bad	*MA⌣oo* (mau)
bananas	*ba-NA-nahss* (bananas)
bandage	*a-ta-DOO-ra* (atadura)
or in Portugal	*lee-ga-DOO-ra* (ligadura)
barber	*bar-BAY-roo* (barbeiro)
bath	*BAHN-yoo* (banho)
beans	*fay-JA⌣oong* (feijão)
bed	*KA-ma* (cama)
beefsteak	*BEE-fee* (bife)
beer	*sayr-VAY-ja* (cerveja)
a glass of beer	*oong KAW-poo dee sayr-VAY-ja* (um copo de cerveja)
blades	
razor blades	*LA-mee-nahss dee jee-LET-ee* (lâminas de gilete)
blankets	*koo-bayr-TAW-reess* (cobertores)
boiled water	*AH-gwa fayr-VEE-da* (agua fervida)

English	Pronunciation and Regular Spelling
Brazilian	*bra-zeel-YAY-roo* (brasileiro)
in Brazilian	*eeng bra-zeel-YAY-roo* (em brasileiro)
bread	*PA‿oong* (pão)
bridge	*PAWN-tee* (ponte)
bring	*TRA-ga* (traga)
Bring help!	*TRA-ga a‿oo-SEEL-yoo!* (Traga auxílio!)
Bring me___	*TRA-ga-mee___* (Traga-me___)
brush	*peen-SEL* (pincel)
shaving brush	*peen-SEL dee BAR-ba* (pincel de barba)
bus	*AW-nee-booss* (ônibus)
butter	*mahn-TAY-ga* (manteiga)
buttons	*boo-TOYNSS* (botões)

C

cabbage	*rray-POHL-yoo* (repolho)
camp	*a-kahm-pa-MEN-too* (acampamento)
can	
I can	*PAW-soo* (Posso)
carrots	*see-NO-rahss* (cenouras)
cheap	*ba-RA-too* (barato)

English	Pronunciation and Regular Spelling
chicken	*FRAHN-goo* (frango)
chocolate	*sho-ko-LA-tee* (chocolate)
church	*ee-GRAY-ja* (igreja)
cigarettes	*see-GA-rrooss* (cigarros)
I want cigarettes	*KEH-roo see-GA-rrooss* (Quero cigarros)
cigars	*sha-ROO-tooss* (charutos)
city	*see-DA-dee* (cidade)
clean	*LEEM-poo* (limpo)
clothing store	*ahl-fa-ya-ta-REE-a* (alfaiataria)
coffee	*ka-FEH* (café)
a cup of coffee	*oo-ma SHEE-ka-ra dee ka-FEH* (uma chicara de café)
cold	*FREE-oo* (frio)
comb	*PEN-tee* (pente)
Come!	*VAYN-ya!* (Venha!)
Come here!	*VAYN-ya KA!* (Venha cá!)
Come quickly!	*VAYN-ya dee-PRESS-a!* (Venha depressa!)
cost	
it costs	*KOO-sta* (custa)
How much does it cost?	*KWAHN-too KOO-sta?* (Quanto custa?)

44

Mateus Place

English	Pronunciation and Regular Spelling
cotton	*ahl-goo-DA͜oong* (algodão)
cover	
Take cover!	*a-BREE-gee-zeel* (Abrigue-se!)
cruzeiro (Brazilian unit of money)	*kroo-ZAY-roo* (cruzeiro)
cucumbers	*pee-PEE-nooss* (pepinos)
cup	*SHEE-ka-ra* (chicara)
a cup of___	*oo-ma SHEE-ka-ra dee___* (uma chicara de___)

45

English	Pronunciation and Regular Spelling

D

Danger!	*pee-REE-gool* (Perigo!)
day	*DEE-a* (dia)
Good day	*bawng DEE-a* (Bom dia)
dentist	*den-TEE-sta* (dentista)
dirty	*SOO-joo* (sujo)
disinfectant	*dee-ZEEN-fay-tahn-tee* (desinfetante)
doctor	*MED-ee-koo* (médico)
Take me to a doctor	*LEV-ee mee ah oong MED-ee-koo* (Leve-me a um médico)
Draw me a map	*day-ZAYN-yee oong MA-pa* (Desenhe um mapa)
drink	*bay-BAYR* (beber)
drugstore	*far-MAHSS-ya* (farmácia)

E

eat	*koo-MAYR* (comer)
I want to eat	*KEH-roo koo-MAYR* (Quero comer)
eggs	*AW-vooss* (óvos)
eight	*OY-too* (oito)
eighteen	*dez-OY-too* (dezoito)
eighty	*oy-TEN-ta* (oitenta)

46

English	Pronunciation and Regular Spelling
eleven	*AWN-zee* (onze)
English	*een-GLAYSS* (inglês)
enough	*ba-STAHN-tee* (bastante)
escudo (Portuguese unit of money)	*ee-SKOO-doo* (escudo)
evening *or* afternoon	*TAR-dee* (tarde)
Good evening	*BO-a TAR-dee* (Boa tarde)
Excuse me	*dee-SKOOL-pee mee* (Desculpe me)
expensive	*KA-roo* (caro)

F

far	*LAWN-jee* (longe)
How far is it?	*ah kee dee-STAHNSS-ya FEE-ka?* (À que distância fica?)
Is it far?	*eh LAWN-jee?* (É longe?)
fifteen	*KEEN-zee* (quinze)
fifty	*seen-KWEN-ta* (cinquenta)
filling station	*PO-stoo dee ga-zo-LEE-na* (pôsto de gasolina)
find	*een-kawn-TRAR* (encontrar)

English	Pronunciation and Regular Spelling
Where can I find___?	*AWN-dee PAW-soo een-kawn-TRAR___?* (Onde posso encontrar___?)
fish	*PAY-shee* (peixe)
five	*SEEN-koo* (cinco)
food	*koo-MEE-da* (comida)
fork	*GAR-foo* (garfo)
forty	*kwa-REN-ta* (quarenta)
four	*KWA-troo* (quatro)
fourteen	*kwa-TAWR-zee* (quatorze)
Friday	*sayss-ta-FAY-ra* (Sexta-Feira)
friend	*a-MEE-goo* (amigo)
I am your friend	*SO a-MEE-goo* (Sou amigo)
fruit	*FROO-tahss* (frutas)

G

garage	*ga-RAHJ* (garage)
Gas!	*GAHSS!* (Gás!)
gasoline	*ga-zo-LEE-na* (gasolina)
get	*awb-TAYR* (obter)
Where can I get___?	*AWN-dee paw-day-RAY awb-TAYR___?* (Onde poderei obter___?)

English	Pronunciation and Regular Spelling
Give me___	*DAY-mee___* (Dê-me___)
glass	*KAW-poo* (copo)
a glass of___	*oong KAW-poo dee___* (um copo de___)
Go!	*VA!* (Vá!)
Go quickly!	*VA dee-PRESS-a!* (Vá depressa!)
good	*BAWNG* (bom)
Good day	*bawng DEE-a* (Bom dia)
Good evening	*BO-a TAR-dee* (Boa tarde)
Good luck	*fee-lee-see-DA-deess* (Felicidades)
Good-by	*a-TEH LAW-goo* (Até logo)
grapes	*OO-vahss* (uvas)
grocery	*VEN-da* (venda)

H

hair	*ka-BAY-loo* (cabelo)
have my hair cut	*kawr-TAR oo ka-BAY-loo* (cortar o cabelo)
half	*MAY-ya* (meia)
half past six	*SAYSS ee MAY-ya* (seis e meia)
ham	*pree-ZOON-too* (presunto)
hot *or* warm	*KEN-tee* (quente)

49

English	Pronunciation and Regular Spelling
handkerchief	*LEN-soo* (lenço)
have	
Have you___?	*TAYNG___?* (Tem___?)
I have___	*TAYN-yoo___* (Tenho___)
I don't have___	*NA⌣oong TAYN-yoo___* (Não tenho___)
We have___	*TAY-mooss___* (Temos___)
We don't have___	*NA⌣oong TAY-mooss___* (Não temos___)
he	*AY-lee* (êle)
He is	*ee-STA___* (Está___)
Help!	*so-KO-rroo!* (Socorro!)
Help me!	*a-JOO-dee mee!* (Ajude-me!)
Bring help!	*TRA-ga a⌣oo-SEEL-yoo!* (Traga auxílio!)
here	*a-KEE* (aquí)
Come here!	*VAYN-ya KA!* (Venha cá!)
highway	*ee-STRA-da preen-see-PAHL* (estrada principal)
hospital	*aw-spee-TAHL* (hospital)
Take me to the hospital	*LEV-ee mee a⌣oo aw-spee-TAHL* (Leve-me ao hospital)

English	Pronunciation and Regular Spelling
hot water	*AH-gwa KEN-tee* (agua quente)
hotel	*o-TEL* (hotel)
Where is a hotel?	*AWN-dee AH oong o-TEL?* (Onde há um hotel?)
house	*KA-za* (casa)
how	*KO-moo* (como)
How do you say___?	*KO-moo see DEESS___?* (Como se diz___?)
How far is it?	*ah kee dee-STAHNSS-ya FEE-ka?* (Á que distância fica?)
How much	*KWAHN-too* (Quanto)
How much does it cost?	*KWAHN-too KOO-sta?* (Quanto custa?)
hundred	*SA YNG* (cem)
hungry	
I am hungry	*ee-STO kawng FAW-mee* (Estou com fome)

I

I	*AY⌣oo* (eu)
I am well	*ee-STO BA YNG* (Estou bem)
I am an American	*SO a-may-ree-KA-noo* (Sou americano)

English	Pronunciation and Regular Spelling
I have___	*TAYN-yoo___* (Tenho___)
I don't have___	*NA⌣oong TAYN-yoo___* (Não tenho___)
I want___ *or* **I want to___**	*KEH-roo___* (Quero___)
I'd like___	*day-ZAY-joo___* (Desejo___)
I will pay you	*AY⌣oo l⌣yee pa-ga-RAY* (Eu lhe pagarei)
ice cream	*sawr-VAY-tee* (sorvête)
in Brazilian	*eeng bra-zeel-YAY-roo* (em brasileiro)
in Portuguese	*eeng pawr-too-GAYSS* (em português)
ink	*TEEN-ta* (tinta)
iodine	*YO-doo* (iodo)
is	
He is sick	*ee-STA DWEN-tee* (Está doente)
Is it expensive?	*ee-STA KA-roo?* (Está caro?)
It is expensive	*ee-STA KA-roo* (Está caro)
Is it far?	*EH LAWN-jee?* (É longe?)
It is near	*EH PAYR-too* (É perto)

52

English	Pronunciation and Regular Spelling
It is not___ *or*	*NA‿oong EH___* (Não é___) *NA‿oong ee-STA___* (Não está___)
What is it?	*oo kee EH?* (O que é?)
Where is it?	*AWN-dee EH?* (Onde é?)
Where is there___?	*AWN-dee AH___?* (Onde há___?)

K

kilometers	*kee-LO-may-trooss*	(quilómetros)
knife	*FA-ka*	(faca)

L

lamb	*kar-NAY-roo*	(carneiro)
large	*GRAHN-dee*	(grande)
laundry	*la-vahn-da-REE-a*	(lavandaria)
laxative	*poor-GAHN-tee*	(purgante)
leave		

At what time does the train leave?   *ah kee AW-rahss SA‿ee oo TRAYNG?*
                                      (A que horas sai o trem?)

English	Pronunciation and Regular Spelling
left	
Turn left	*VEE-ree ah ee-SKAYR-da* (Vire à esquerda)
lemons	*lee-MOYNSS* (limões)
lettuce	*ahl-FA-see* (alface)
like	
I'd like___	*day-ZAY-joo___* (Desejo___)
lost	*payr-DEE-doo* (perdido)
luck	
Good luck	*fee-lee-see-DA-deess* (Felicidades)

M

English	Pronunciation and Regular Spelling
Madam *or* Mrs.	*sayn-YAW-ra* (Senhora)
main street	*RROO-a preen-see-PAHL* (rua principal)
mangos	*MAHN-gahss* (mangas)
map	*MA-pa* (mapa)
Draw me a map	*day-ZAYN-yee oong MA-pa* (Desenhe um mapa)
market	*mayr-KA-doo* (mercado)
matches	*FAW-sfaw-rooss* (fósforos)

English	Pronunciation and Regular Spelling
mattress	*kawl-SHA⌣oong* (colchão)
me	*mee* (me)
meat	*KAR-nee* (carne)
mechanic	*may-KA-nee-koo* (mecânico)
milk	*LAY-tee* (leite)
milréis (old Brazilian unit of money)	*meel-RRAYSS* (milréis)
minute	
Wait a minute!	*ee-SPEH-roo oong een-STAHN-tee!* (Espere um instante!)
Miss	*sayn-yo-REE-ta* (Senhorita)
Mister	*sayn-YAWR* (Senhor)
Monday	*see-goon-da-FAY-ra* (Segunda-Feira)
mosquito net	*mooss-kee-TAY-roo* (mosquiteiro)
movie	*see-NAY-ma* (cinema)
At what time does the movie start?	*ah-kee AW-rahss koo-MESS-a oo see-NAY-ma?* (A que horas começa o cinema?)
much	*MOO⌣een-too* (muito)

English	Pronunciation and Regular Spelling

N

name

    My name is___   *may‿oo NO-mee EH___*   (Meu nome é___)

    What is your name?   *KO-moo see SHA-ma?*   (Como se chama?)

near   *PAYR-too*   (perto)

    the nearest town   *ah see-DA-dee MA‿eess PRAW-see-ma*
                             (a cidade mais próxima)

needle   *a-GOOL-ya*   (agulha)

nine   *NAW-vee*   (nove)

nineteen   *dee-zeh-NAW-vee*   (dezenove)

ninety   *naw-VEN-ta*   (noventa)

no *or* not   *NA‿oong*   (não)

north   *NAWR-tee*   (norte)

    Which way is north?   *dee kee LA-doo EH oo NAWR-tee?*
                             (De que lado é o norte?)

O

of   *dee*   (de)
         or   *djee*   (de)

National Coach Museum, Lisbon

Belem Tower, Lisbon

English	Pronunciation and Regular Spelling
a cup of coffee	*oo-ma SHEE-ka-ra dee ka-FEH* (uma chicara de café)
a glass of beer	*oong KAW-poo dee sayr-VAY-ja* (um copo de cerveja)
quarter of two	*oong KWAR-too pa-ra ahz DOO-ahss* (um quarto para as duas)
ten minutes of three	*DAYSS pa-ra ahss TRAYSS* (dez para as três)
one	*OONG* (um)
onions	*see-BO-lahss* (cebôlas)
oranges	*la-RAHN-jahss* (laranjas)

P

paper	*pa-PEL* (papel)
past	
half past six	*SAYSS ee MAY-ya* (seis e meia)
quarter past five	*SEEN-koo ee oong KWAR-too* (cinco e um quarto)
pay	
I will pay you	*AY⌣oo l⌣yee pa-ga-RAY* (Eu lhe pagarei)
peas	*ayr-VEEL-yahss* (ervilhas)
pen	*ka-NET-a* (caneta)

English	Pronunciation and Regular Spelling
pencil	*LA-peess* (lápis)
pepper	*pee-MEN-ta* (pimenta)
pillow	*tra-vee-SAY-roo* (travesseiro)
pineapple	*a-BA-ka-shee* (abacaxi)
or	*AH-na-nahss* (ananás)
pins	*ahl-fee-NAY-tee* (alfinete)
safety pins	*ahl-fee-NAY-tee dee see-goo-RAHN-sa* (alfinete de segurança)
pipe	*ka-SHEEM-boo* (cachimbo)
plate	*PRA-too* (prato)
please	*pawr fa-VAWR* (por favor)
Point!	*MAW-streel* (Mostre!)
policeman	*poo-LEESS-ya* (polícia)
police station	*day-lay-ga-SEE-a dee poo-LEESS-ya* (delegacia de polícia)
polish	
shoe polish	*GRA-sha dee sa-PA-too* (graxa de sapato)
pork	*PAWR-koo* (porco)
porter	*ka-rreh-ga-DAWR* (carregador)

English	Pronunciation and Regular Spelling
Portuguese	*pawr-too-GAYSS* (português)
in Portuguese	*eeng pawr-too-GAYSS* (em português)
post office	*kaw-RRAY-oo* (correio)
potatoes	*ba-TA-tahss* (batatas)

Q

quarter	*KWAR-too* (quarto)
quarter of two	*oong KWAR-too pa-ra ahz DOO-ahss* (um quarto para as duas)
quickly	*dee-PRESS-a* (depressa)
Come quickly!	*VAYN-ya dee-PRESS-a!* (Venha depressa!)
Go quickly!	*VA dee-PRESS-a!* (Vá depressa!)

R

railroad	*ee-STRA-da dee FEH-rroo* (estrada de ferro)
Where is a railroad?	*AWN-dee EH ah ee-STRA-da dee FEH-rroo?* (Onde é a estrada de ferro?)

English	Pronunciation and Regular Spelling
railroad station	*ee-sta-SA͜oong* (estação)
raincoat	*eem-payr-may-AH-vel* (impermeável)
razor	*na-VAHL-ya* (navalha)
razor blades	*LA-mee-nahss dee jee-LET-ee* (lâminas de gilete)
rest	*dee-skahn-SAR* (desçansar)
restaurant	*rray-sto-RAHNG* (restaurant)
Where is a restaurant?	*AWN-dee AH oong rray-sto-RAHNG?* (Onde há um restaurant?)
rice	*a-RROYSS* (arroz)
right	
Turn right	*VEE-ree ah dee-RAY-ta* (Vire à direita)
river	*RREE-o* (rio)
road	*ee-STRA-da* (estrada)
room	*KWAR-too* (quarto)

English	Pronunciation and Regular Spelling

S

safety pins	*ahl-fee-NAY-tee dee see-goo-RAHN-sa* (alfinete de segurança)
salad	*sa-LA-da* (salada)
salt	*SAHL* (sal)
Saturday	*SA-ba-doo* (Sábado)
say	
How do you say___?	*KO-moo see DEESS___?* (Como se diz___?)
servant	*kree-AH-doo* (criado)
seven	*SET-ee* (sete)
seventeen	*djee-zeh-SET-ee* (dezessete)
seventy	*seh-TEN-ta* (setenta)
shave	
be shaved	*fa-ZAYR ah BAR-ba* (fazer a barba)
shaving brush	*peen-SEL dee BAR-ba* (pincel de barba)
shaving soap	*sa-BA⏝oong dee BAR-ba* (sabão de barba)
she	*EL-a* (ela)
sheets	*len-SOYSS* (lençóis)
shirt	*ka-MEE-za* (camisa)

English	Pronunciation and Regular Spelling
shoemaker	*sa-pa-TAY-roo* (sapateiro)
shoes	*sa-PA-tooss* (sapatos)
shoe laces	*kawr-DOYNSS dee sa-PA-tooss* (cordões de sapatos)
shoe polish	*GRA-sha dee sa-PA-too* (graxa de sapato)
sick	*DWEN-tee* (doente)
Sir	*sayn-YAWR* (Senhor)
six	*SAYSS* (seis)
sixteen	*djee-zeh-SAYSS* (dezesseis)
sixty	*seh-SEN-ta* (sessenta)
sleep	*door-MEER* (dormir)
slowly	*dee-va-GAR* (devagar)
Speak slowly	*FA-lee dee-va-GAR* (Fale devagar)
small	*pee-KEW-oo* (pequeno)
soap	*sa-BA‿oong* (sabão)
soup	*SO-pa* (sôpa)

Lisbon

English	Pronunciation and Regular Spelling
Speak!	*FA-lee!* (Fale!)
he speaks	*FA-la* (fala)
Speak slowly	*FA-lee dee-va-GAR* (Fale devagar)
spoon	*kool-YA YR* (colher)
spring	*FA WN-tee* (fonte)
start	
At what time does the movie start?	*ah kee A W-rahss koo-MEH-sa oo see-NA Y-ma?* (A que horas começa o cinema?)
station	
police station	*day-lay-ga-SEE-a dee poo-LEESS-ya* (delegacia de polícia)
railroad station	*ee-sta-SA̲oong* (estação)
steak	
beefsteak	*BEE-fee* (bife)
Stop!	*PA-ree!* (Pare!)
store	
clothing store	*ahl-fa-ya-ta-REE-a* (alfaiataria)
drugstore	*far-MAHSS-ya* (farmácia)

English	Pronunciation and Regular Spelling
Straight ahead	*SEE-ga eeng FREN-chee* (Siga em frente)
street	*RROO-a* (rua)
main street	*RROO-a preen-see-PAHL* (rua principal)
street car	*BAWN-dee* (bonde)
or in Portugal	*ee-LET-ree-koo* (elétrico)
sugar	*a-SOO-kar* (açúcar)
Sunday	*doo-MEEN-goo* (Domingo)

T

tailor	*ahl-fa-YA-tee* (alfaiate)
take	
Take cover!	*a-BREE-gee-zee!* (Abrigue-se!)
Take me there	*LEV-ee-mee a-TEH LA* (Leve-me até lá)
Take me to a doctor	*LEV-ee-mee ah oong MED-ee-ko* (Leve-me a um médico)
Take me to the hospital	*LEV-ee-mee a‿oo aw-spee-TAHL* (Leve-me ao hospital)
tea	*SHA* (chá)
telegraph office	*tay-LEG-ra-foo* (telégrafo)
telephone	*tay-lay-FAW-nee* (telefóne)
ten	*DAYSS* (dez)

English	Pronunciation and Regular Spelling
Thank you	*o-bree-GA-doo* (Obrigado)
that	*a-KEE-loo* (aquilo)
What is that?	*o kee EH a-KEE-loo?* (O que é aquilo?)
the	*oo* (o)
or	*ah* (a)
or	*ooss* (os)
or	*ahss* (as)
there	*a-LEE* (alí)
Take me there	*LEV-ee-mee a-TEH LA* (Leve-me até lá)
they	*AY-leess* (êles)
thirsty	*kawng SAY-dee* (com sêde)
thirteen	*TRAY-zee* (treze)
thirty	*TREEN-ta* (trinta)
this	*EE-stoo* (isto)
thousand	*MEEL* (mil)
thread	*LEEN-ya* (linha)
three	*TRAYSS* (três)
Thursday	*keen-ta-FAY-ra* (Quinta-Feira)
time	
At what time?	*ah kee AW-rahss?* (A que horas?)
What time is it?	*kee AW-rahss SA‿oong?* (Que horas são?)

English	Pronunciation and Regular Spelling
tired	*kahn-SA-doo* (cançado)
to	*ah* (a)
to a doctor	*ah oong MED-ee-ko* (a um médico)
to the hospital	*a‿oo aw-spee-TAHL* (ao hospital)
tobacco	*FOO-moo* (fumo)
or	*ta-BA-koo* (tabaco)
today	*O-jee* (hoje)
toilet	*pree-VA-da* (privada)
Where is a toilet?	*AWN-dee EH ah pree-VA-da?* (Onde é a privada?)
tomatoes	*to-MA-teess* (tomates)
tomorrow	*a-mahn-YAHNG* (amanhã)
too	*MOO‿een-too* (muito)
toothbrush	*ee-SKO-va dee DEN-teess* (escova de dentes)
tooth paste	*PA-sta pa-ra DEN-teess* (pasta para dentes)
towel	*TWAHL-ya* (toalha)
town	
the nearest town	*ah see-DA-dee MA‿eess PRAW-see-ma* (a cidade mais próxima)

English	Pronunciation and Regular Spelling
train	*TRAYNG* (trem)
or in Portugal	*kawm-BOY-oo* (comboio)
When does the train leave?	*ah kee AW-rahss SA⌣ee oo TRAYNG?* (A que horas sai o trem?)
Tuesday	*tehr-sa-FAY-ra* (Terça-Feira)
Turn!	*VEE-reel!* (Vire!)
Turn left	*VEE-ree ah ee-SKAYR-da* (Vire à esquerda)
Turn right	*VEE-ree ah dee-RAY-ta* (Vire à direita)
twelve	*DO-zee* (doze)
twenty	*VEEN-tee* (vinte)
twenty-one	*VEEN-tee ee OONG* (vinte e um)
twenty-two	*VEEN-tee ee DOYSS* (vinte e dois)
two	*DOYSS* (dois)

U

undershirt	*ka-mee-ZAY-ta* (camiseta)
undershorts	*KWEK-ahss* (cuécas)
understand	
I don't understand	*NA⌣oong een-TEN-doo* (Não entendo)

English	Pronunciation and Regular Spelling
Understand me?	*een-TEN-dee mee?* (Entende me?)
until	*a-TEH* (até)
until tomorrow	*a-TEH a-mahn-YAHNG* (até amanhã)

V

veal	*vee-TEL-a* (vitela)
vegetables	*vej-eh-TA͜eess* (vegetais)
very	*MOO͜een-too* (muito)
village	*VEE-la* (vila)

W

Wait a minute!	*ee-SPEH-roo oong een-STAHN-teel* (Espere um instante!)
want	
I want___ *or* I want to___	*KEH-roo___* (Quero___)
We want___	*kay-RAY-mooss___* (Queremos___)
warm or hot	*KEN-tee* (quente)
wash	*la-VAR* (lavar)

English	Pronunciation and Regular Spelling
Watch out!	*a-ten-SA⁀oong!* (Atenção!)
water	*AH-gwa* (água)
boiled water	*AH-gwa fayr-VEE-da* (agua fervida)
hot water	*AH-gwa KEN-tee* (agua quente)
we	*NOYSS* (nós)
We are___	*ee-STA-mooss___* (Estamos___)
We have___	*TAY-mooss___* (Temos___)
We don't have___	*NA⁀oong TAY-mooss___* (Não temos___)
We want___	*kay-RAY-mooss___* (Queremos___)
Wednesday	*kwar-ta-FAY-ra* (Quarta-Feira)
well (in good health)	*BAYNG* (bem)
well (for water)	*PO-soo* (pôço)
what	*KEE* (que)
At what time?	*ah kee AW-rahss?* (A que horas?)
What is that?	*o kee EH a-KEE-loo?* (O que é aquilo?)
What is your name?	*KO-moo see SHA-ma?* (Como se chama?)

English	Pronunciation and Regular Spelling
What time is it?	*kee AW-rahss SA⌣oong?* (Que horas são?)
where	*AWN-dee* (onde)
Where are they?	*AWN-dee ee-STA⌣oong?* (Onde estão?)
Where is it?	*AWN-dee EH?* (Onde é?)
Where is there___?	*AWN-dee AH___?* (Onde há___?)
Where can I find___?	*AWN-dee PAW-soo een-kawn-TRAR___?* (Onde posso encontrar___?)
Where can I get___?	*AWN-dee paw-day-RAY awb-TAYR___?* (Onde poderei obter___?)
which	*KWAHL* (qual)
Which is the road to___?	*KWAHL EH ah ee-STRA-da pa-ra___?* (Qual é a estrada para___?)
Which way is north?	*dee kee LA-doo EH oo NAWR-tee?* (De que lado é o norte?)
wine	*VEEN-yoo* (vinho)
workman	*tra-bahl-ya-DAWR* (trabalhador)
wounded	*fee-REE-doo* (ferido)
Write it!	*ee-SKRAY-va-o!* (Escreva-o!)

70

English	Pronunciation and Regular Spelling

Y

yes	*SEENG* (sim)
you	*vo-SAY* (você)
Are you___?	*ee-STA___?* (Está___?)
Have you___?	*TAYNG___?* (Tem___?)
I will pay you	*AY⏝oo l⏝yee pa-ga-RAY* (Eu lhe pagarei)

River Douro

National Palace of Queluz